girlfriends forever

We've got each other's back

REEDA JOSEPH

VIVA
EDITIONS

Published in the United States by Viva Editions, an imprint of
Cleis Press, Inc., 2246 Sixth Street, Berkeley, California 94710.

Printed in China.
Cover design: Scott Idleman/Blink
Cover photograph: Wright Card Co.
Text design: Tracy Johnson and Frank Wiedemann
First Edition.
10 9 8 7 6 5 4 3 2 1

ISBN: 978-1-936740-21-5

Library of Congress Cataloging-in-Publication Data
available on request.

Dear Reader,

Why is it that bars and clubs feature "Ladies' Night" only once a week, I ask you? I think every night should be Ladies' Night! I have solved my own (and quite of few of the world's) problems over a martini with my gal pals. Haven't you? Girlfriends are like the hot bath you look forward to at the end of the day: all your worries and stresses disappear as you laugh and gossip with your besties about the latest things going on in your life.

I have gathered some of my favorite "vintage vixen" images to celebrate the bonds of true friendship in *Girlfriends Forever*. Of course, I added my own special advice. Speaking of which, here are some brilliant words from two wise and witty women:

> "It's the friends you can call up at 4 am that matter."
> —Marlene Dietrich

> "I can trust my friends. These people force me to examine myself, encourage me to grow."
> —Cher

No balm to salve an upset and no fireworks to celebrate a success equal the support of a true friend. So go ahead, gather your closest gal pals, and share a Ladies' Night filled with love, laughter, and connection. Cherish your *Girlfriends Forever*!

Reeda

I think we get along so well because we are both bitches

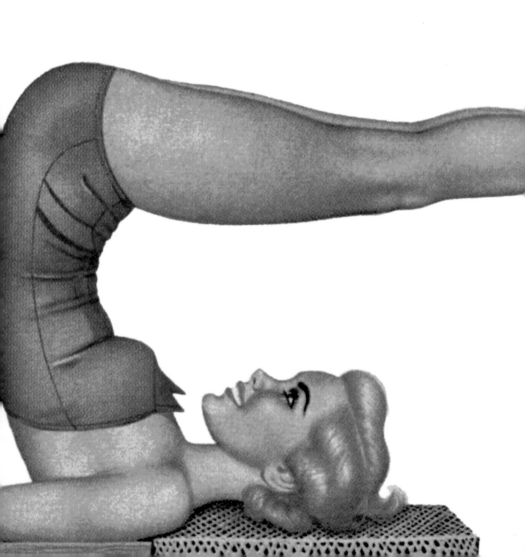

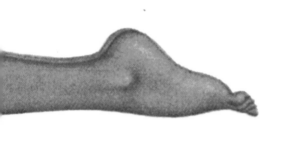

If you've got it, flaunt it!

Nice place
to work

... BUT THE TIPS SUCK.

Roses may be romantic . . .
but **JEWELRY** is much more practical.

*I remember when
I believed everything he told me*

You can say I took my divorce well!

I can barely breathe in this damn dress...

BUT I LOOK FABULOUS

OF COURSE THEY'RE REAL...

I have the receipt to prove it.

I
NEED
A DAY
OFF!

What would I have done without my

MOTHER?

Probably had a much happier childhood!

HAPPY BIRTHDAY

from one bitch to another

OH NO!

I've turned into my mother

Sure I cheated first...
I've always been a TRENDSETTER.

Don't let the apron fool you . . .

I'm not wearing any underwear.

SURE, I HAVE RULES...

but life is more fun when you leave them at home.

When life gives you lemons...

The hell with lemonade.

Okay,
there's a reason why they call it a

Phone.

It's so important to me to always get my family's towels soft and fluffy . . .

. . . NOT!

Being a bad cook was
the smartest move
I ever made...

He's always insisting
we go out to dinner.

Tax

Total

Thank You — Please Come Again

I had another naughty dream last night . . .
guess who **wasn't** *in it?*

Marriage is finding that one special person to **ANNOY** for the rest of your life.

**IF YOU
THINK**
I'm being difficult
NOW
...just wait!

I might look innocent…
but trust me,
I'm guilty of plenty.

I started to act real sweet toward Grandma when I learned what the word **"INHERITANCE"** meant.

another

BIRTHDAY

what a drag.

HUBBY'S
AT WORK,
the kids
are at school,

*and I have just a few hours to myself
until I have to act excited to see them again!*

Bitches

don't talk behind your back

THEY SAY IT TO YOUR FACE!

Sure, blondes have more fun . . .

**as long as they don't have
two kids,
a husband,
and a ton of dirty laundry.**

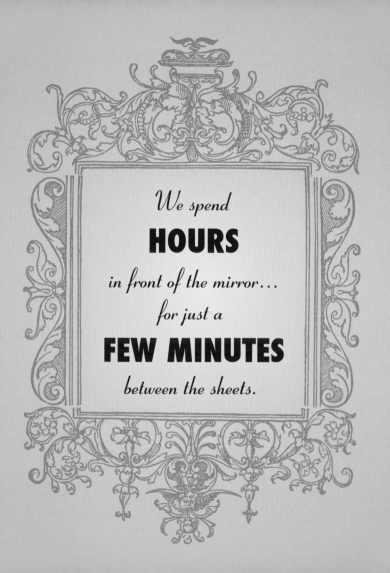

We spend

HOURS

in front of the mirror…

for just a

FEW MINUTES

between the sheets.

Don't let the **sweet and innocent** *act fool you. Remember...* *you can't judge a* **bitch** *by her cover.*

What's wrong with my attitude?
It matches my outfit.

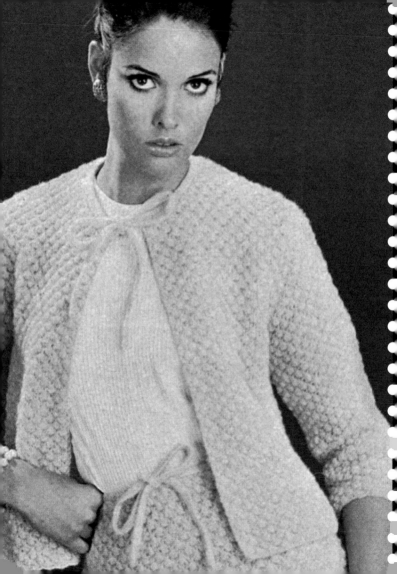

1

SINCE
NICE GIRLS
FINISH
LAST

. . . I intend to be first over the finish line.

*My mother has always been
my best friend...*

it's a shame she annoys the hell out of me.

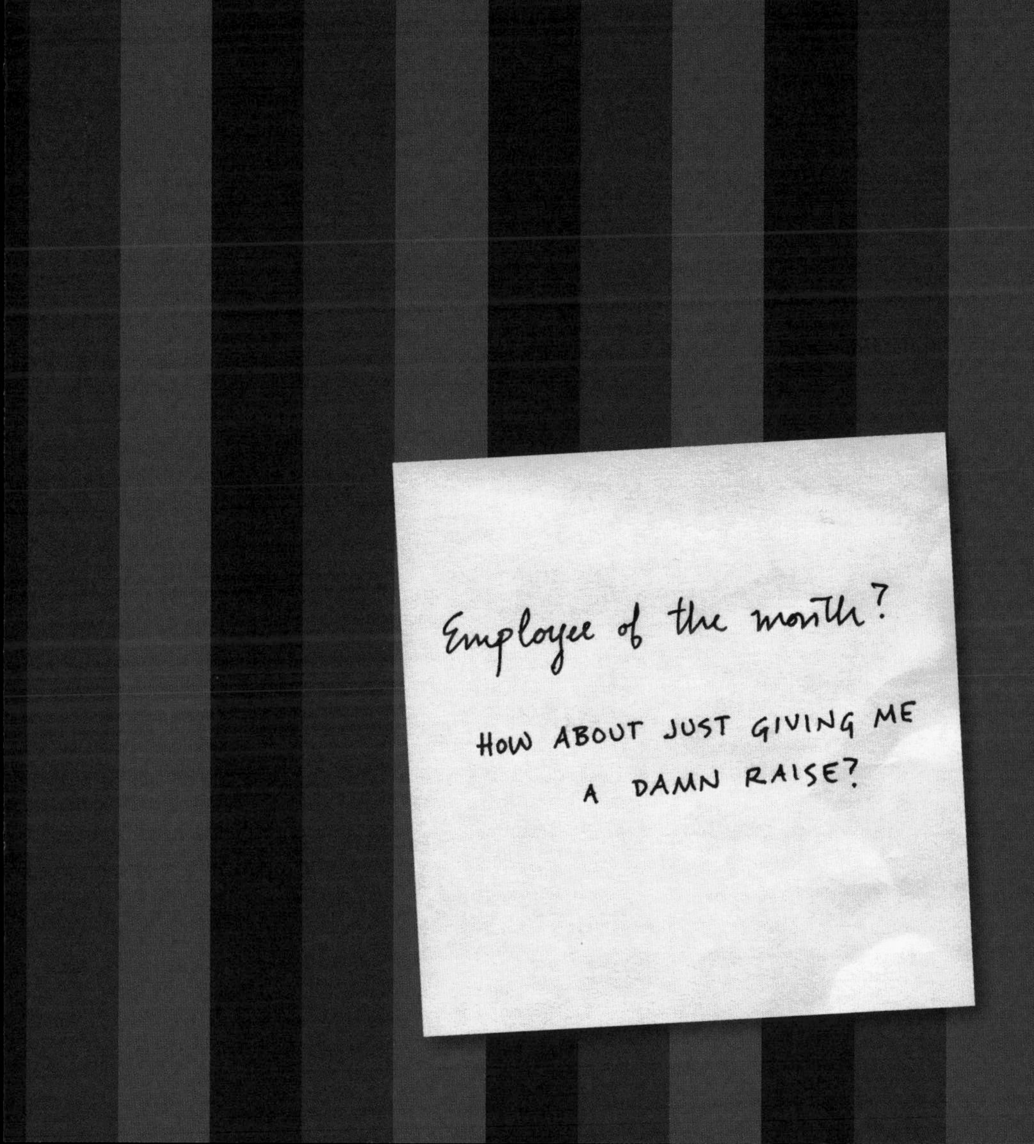
Employee of the month?
HOW ABOUT JUST GIVING ME A DAMN RAISE?

It's true beauty is only skin deep,

'cause I have some pretty ugly thoughts.

Sure sex is a weapon...

AND I'M LOADED!

REYNOLDS WRAP *Pure Aluminum* FOIL

ABOUT THE AUTHOR

Reeda Joseph has been a collector of one-of-a-kind nostalgic items since childhood. From church basements to garage sales to the flea markets of Paris, Reeda is constantly searching for (and finding) vintage images. A designer of cards and stationery for WrightCardCo.com, she lives in San Francisco, California.